Dot Markers

Activity Book

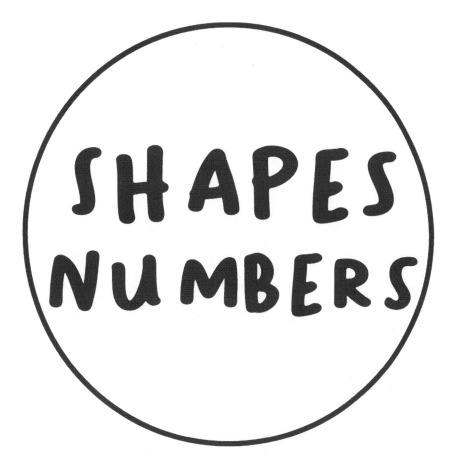

SHAPES
NUMBERS

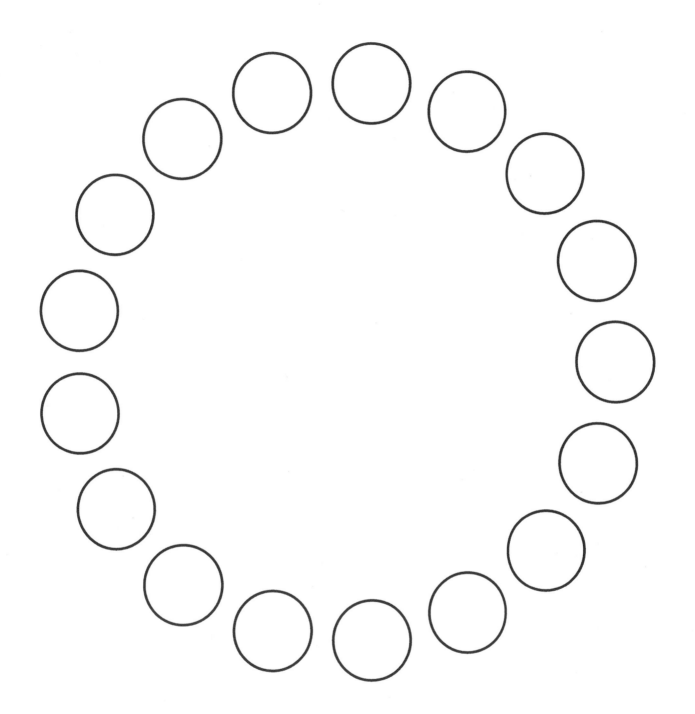

CIRCLE

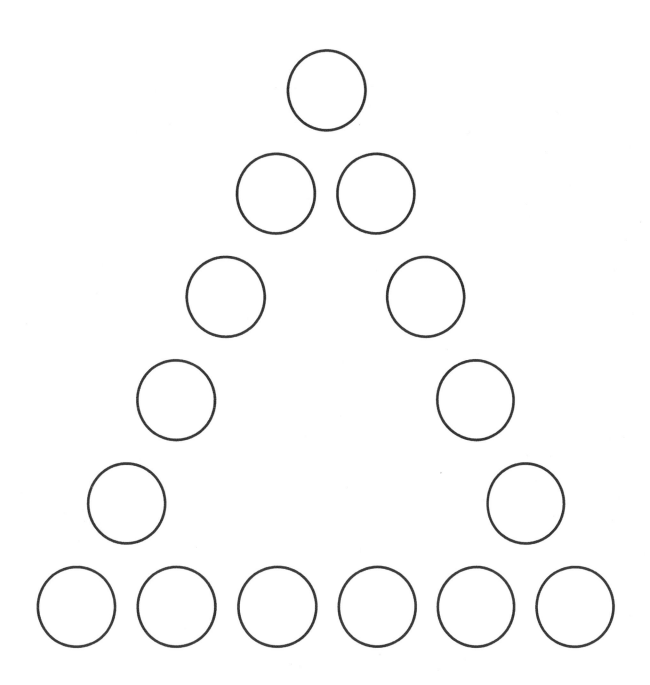

TRIANGLE

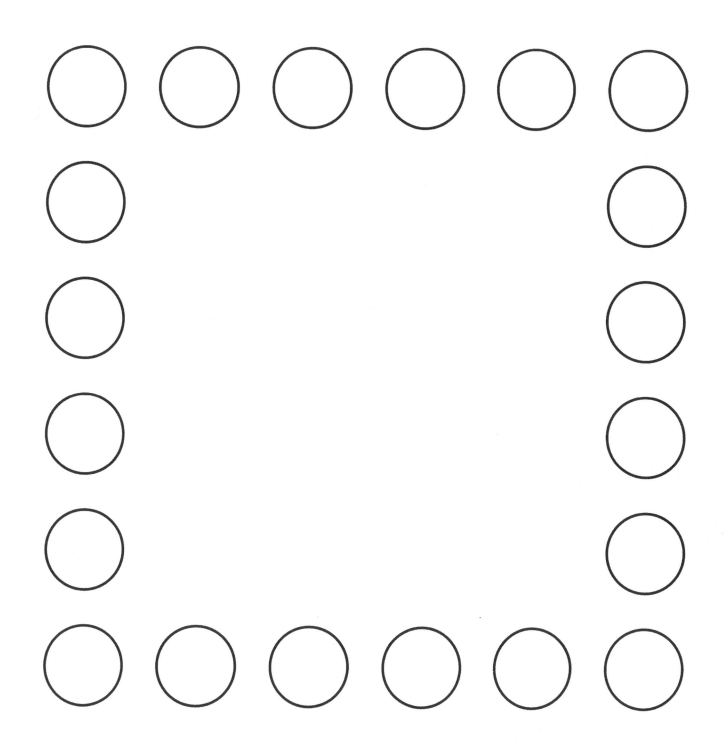

SQUARE

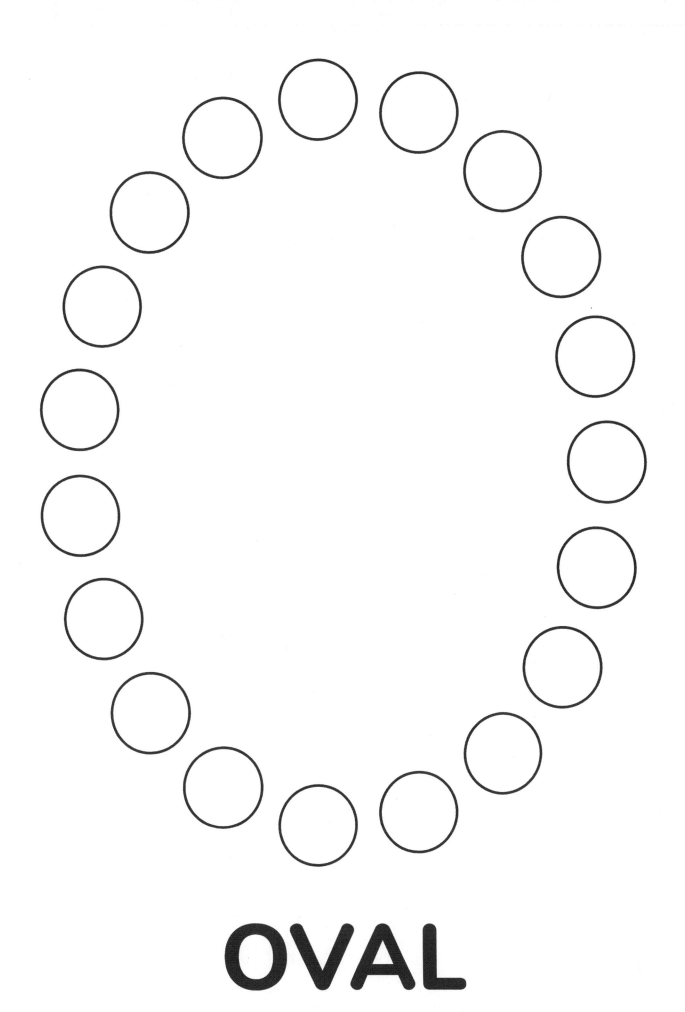

OVAL

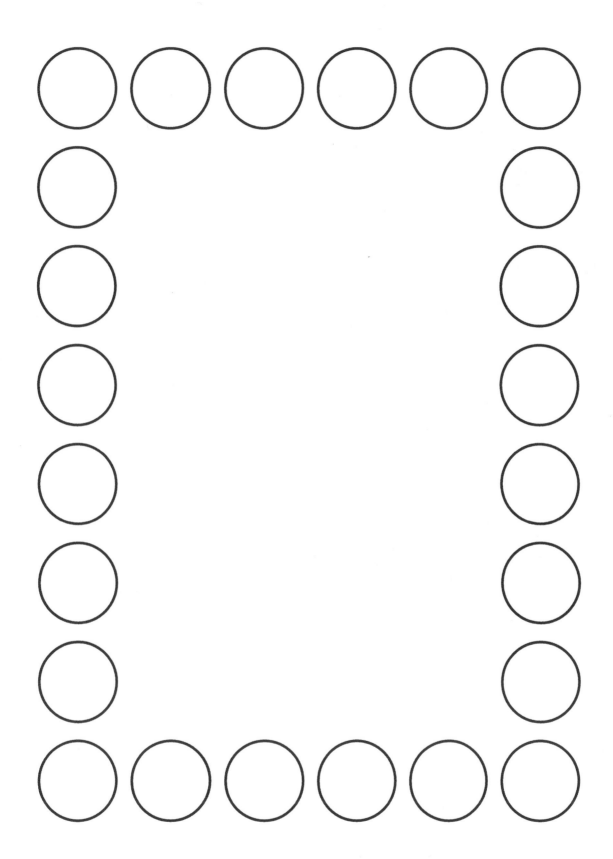

RECTANGLE

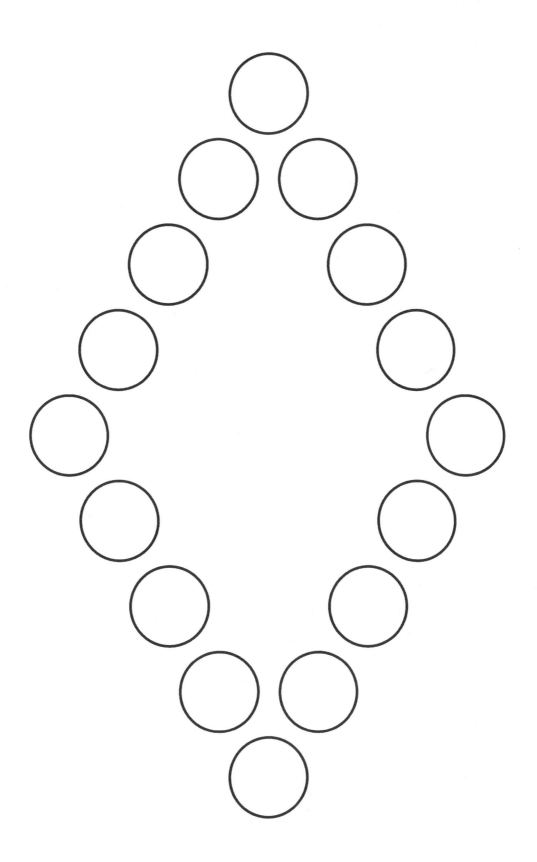

DIAMOND

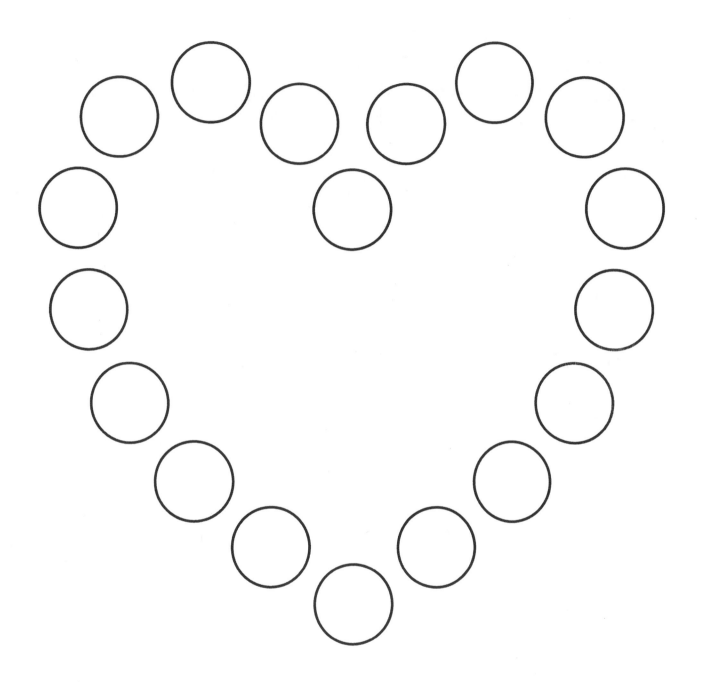

HEART

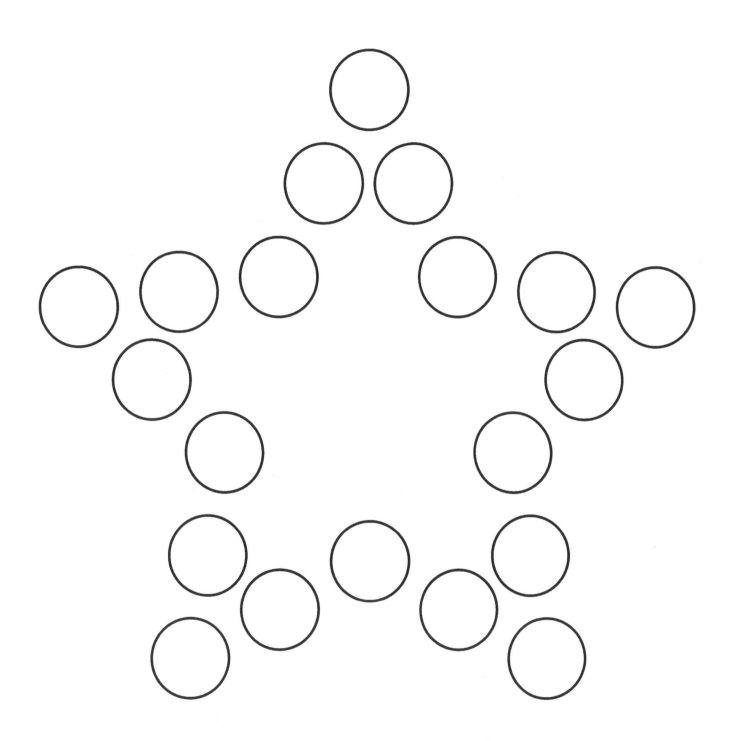

STAR

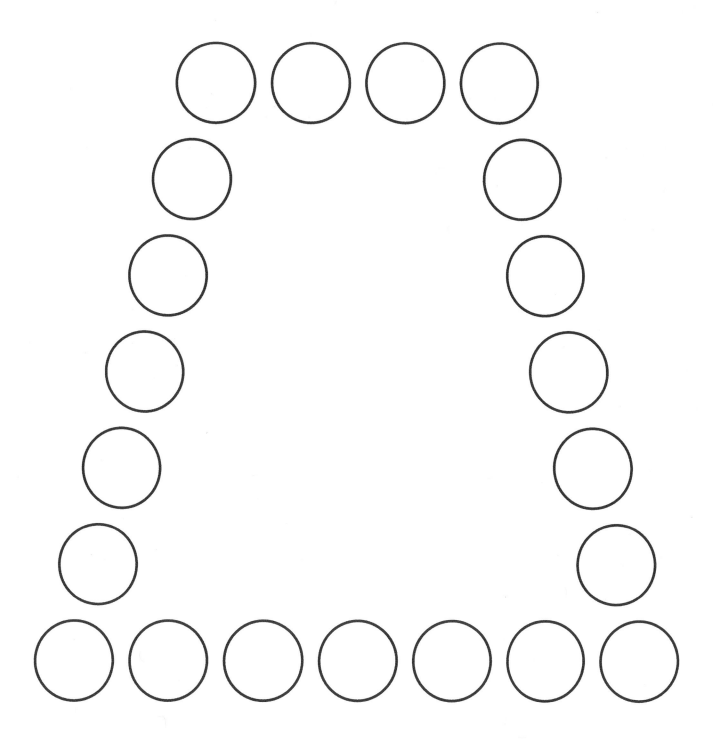

TRAPEZOID

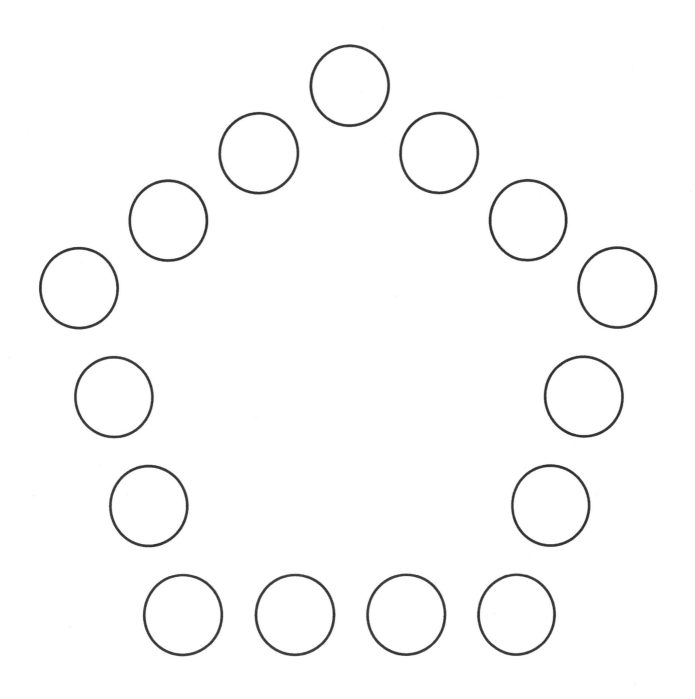

PENTAGON

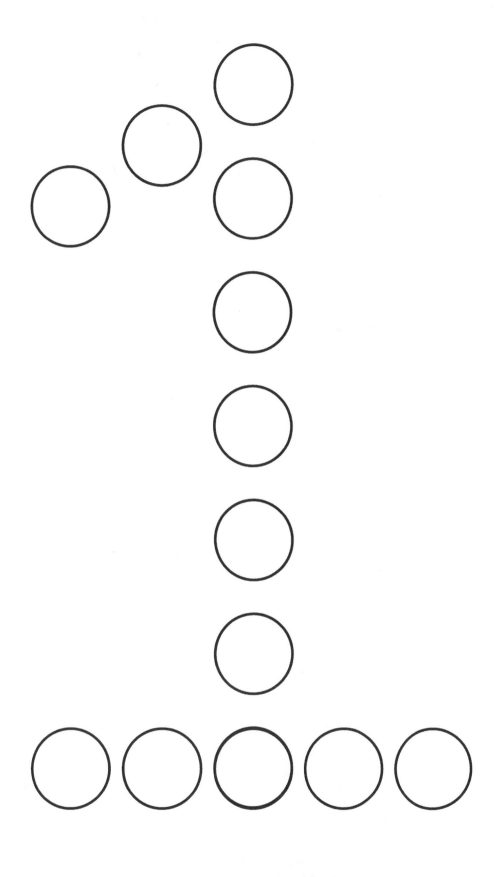

ONE

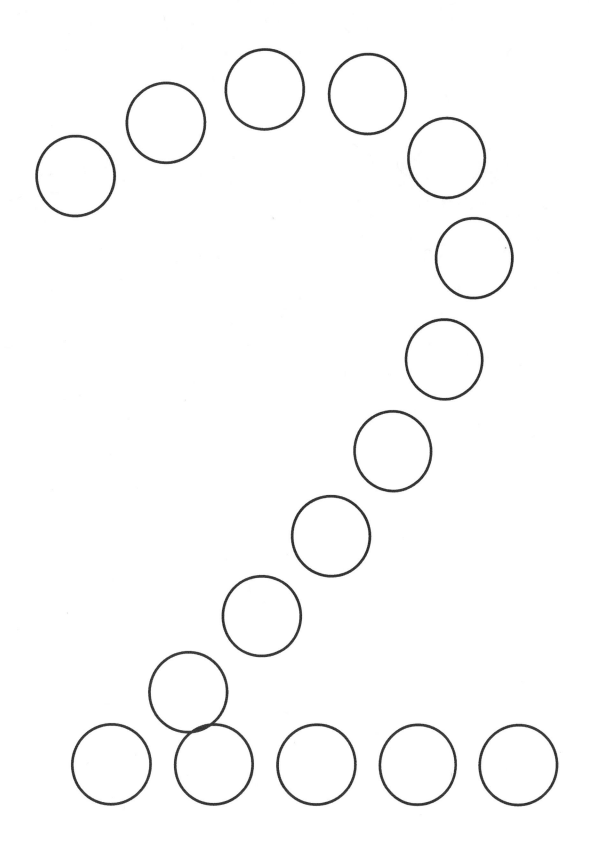

TWO

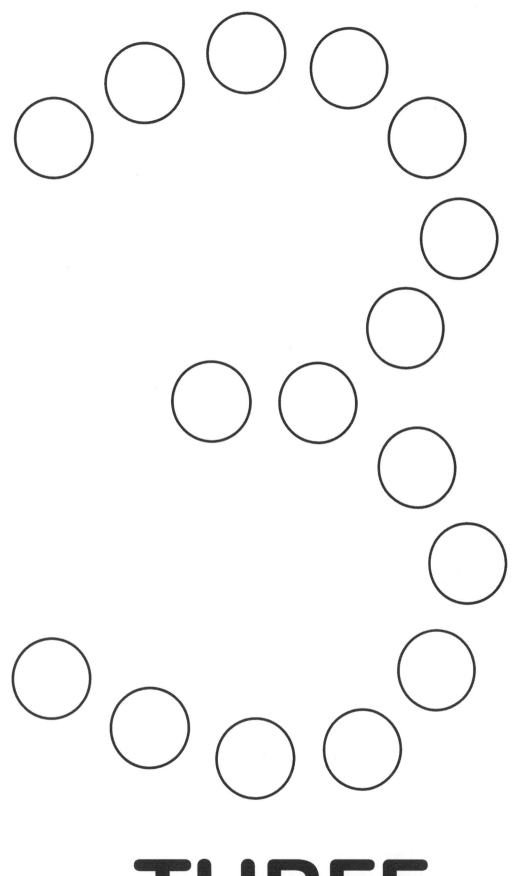

THREE

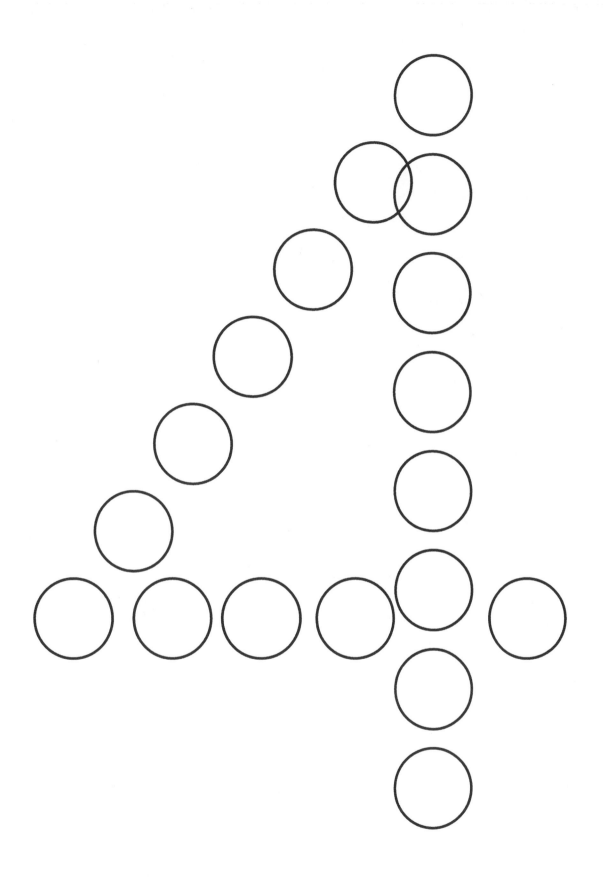

FOUR

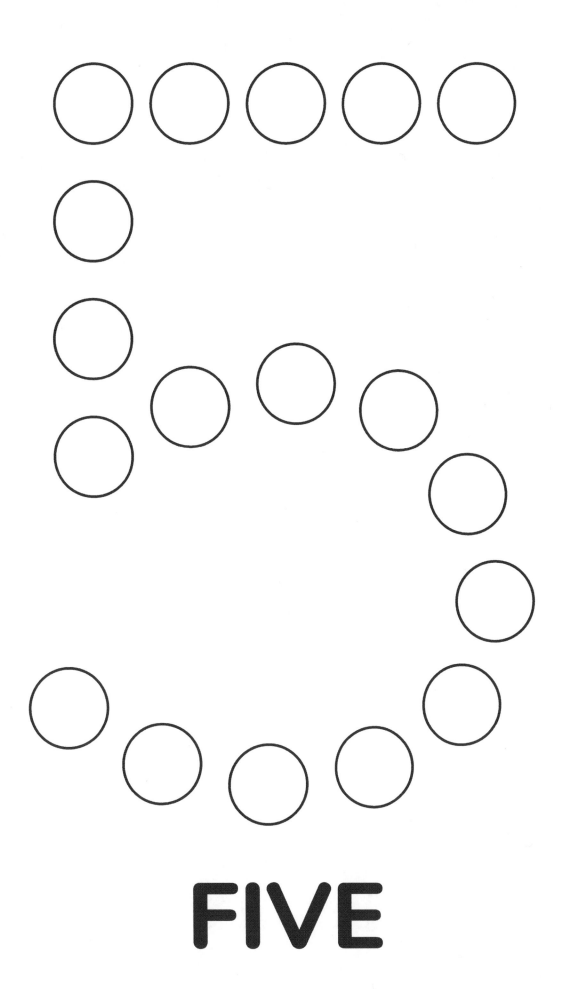

FIVE

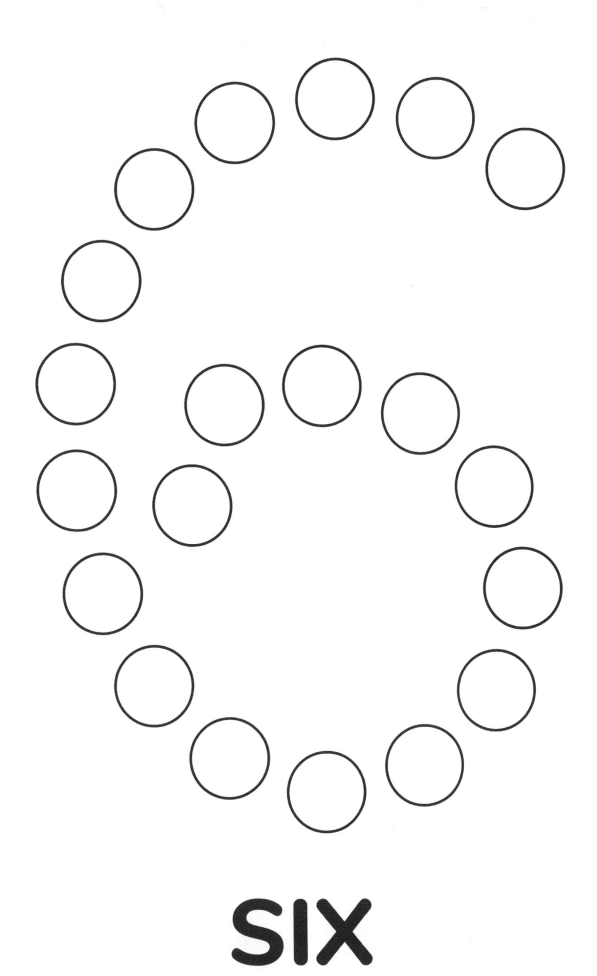

SIX

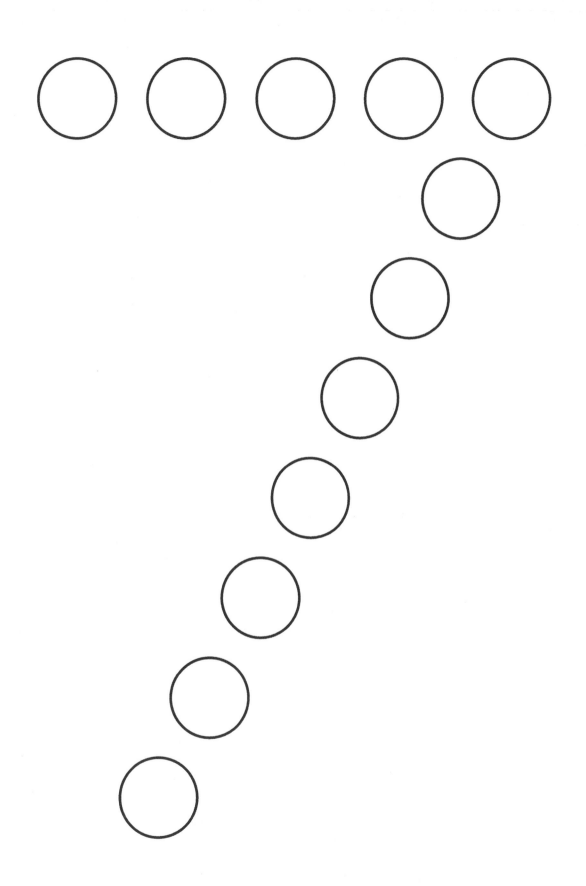

SEVEN

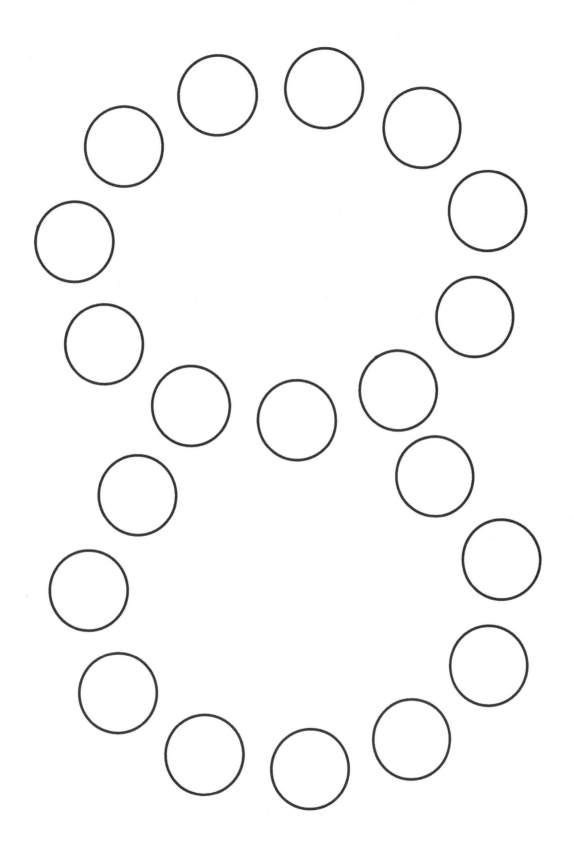

EIGHT

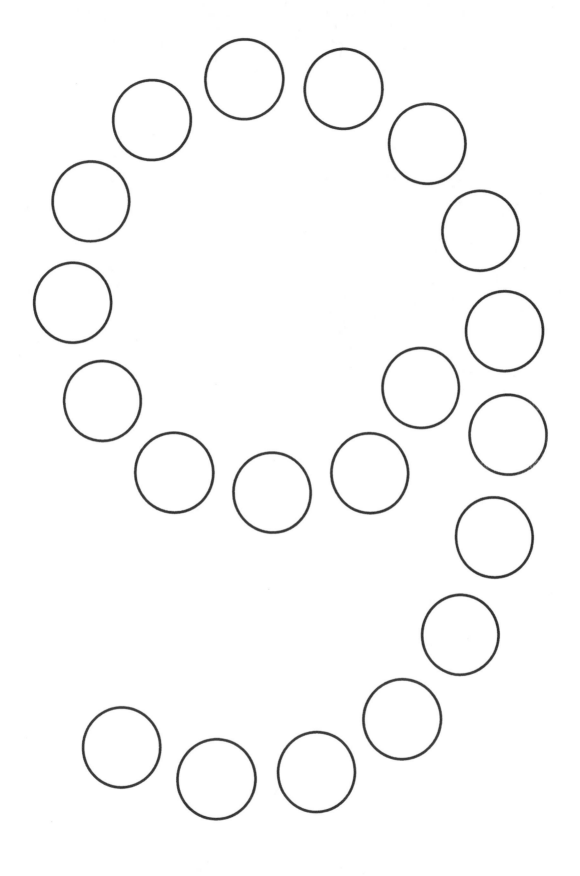

NINE

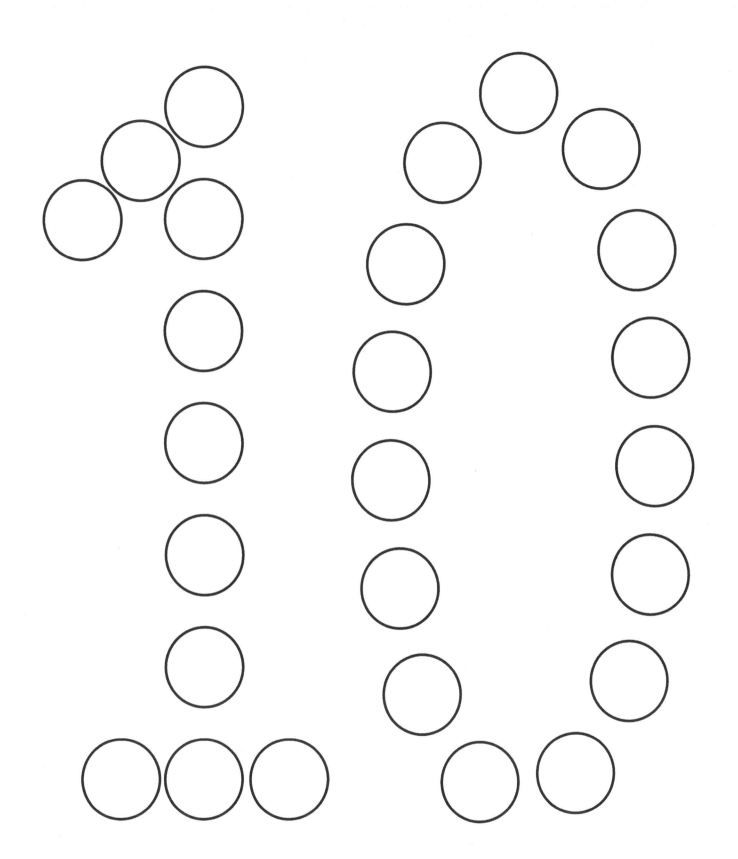

TEN

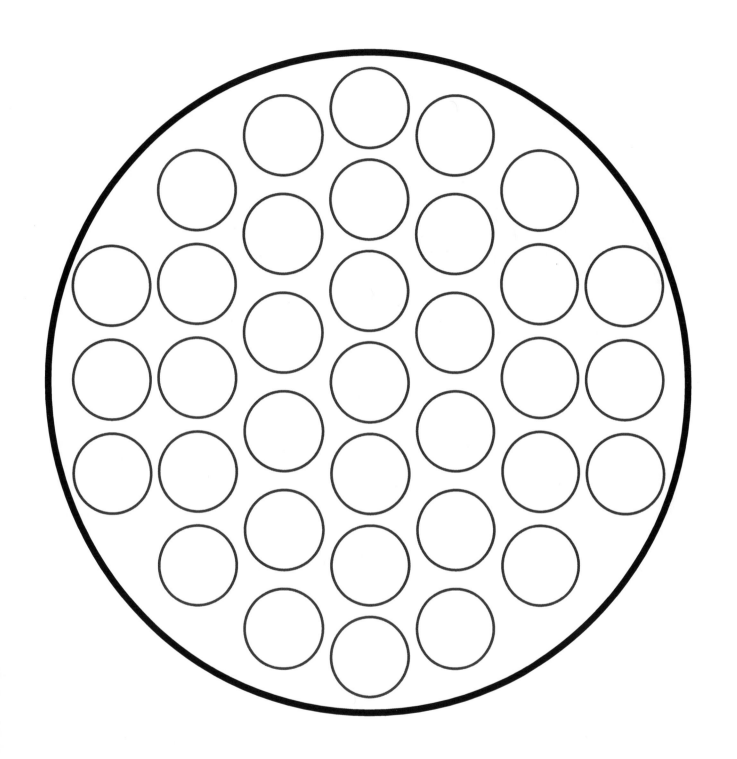

CIRCLE

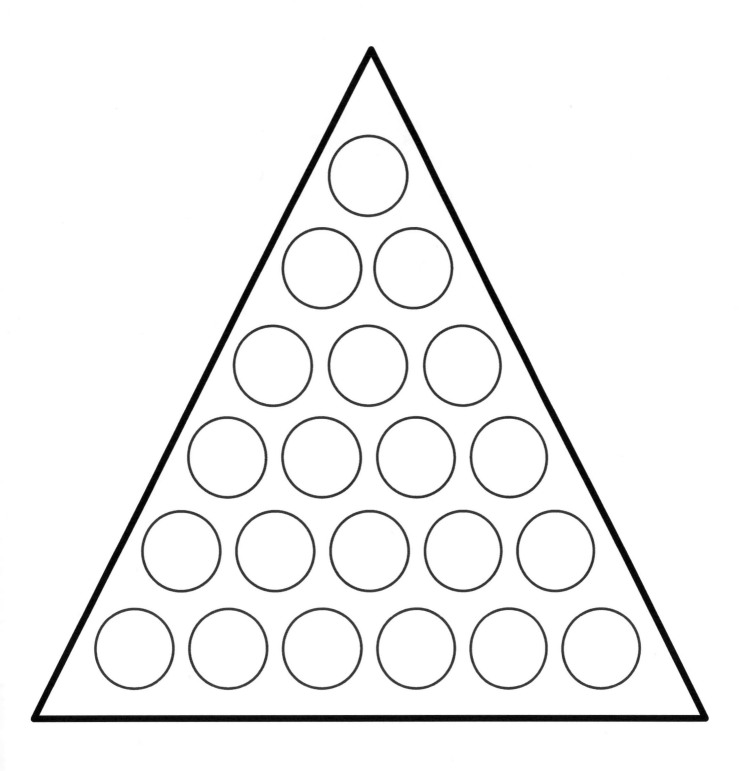

TRIANGLE

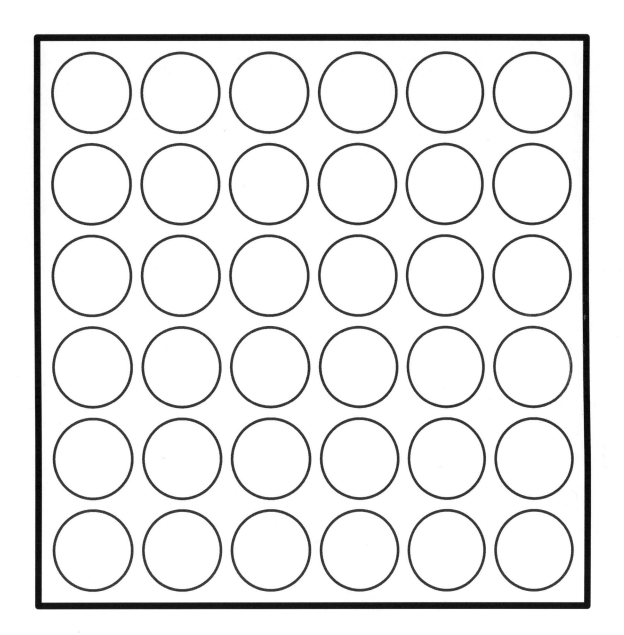

SQUARE

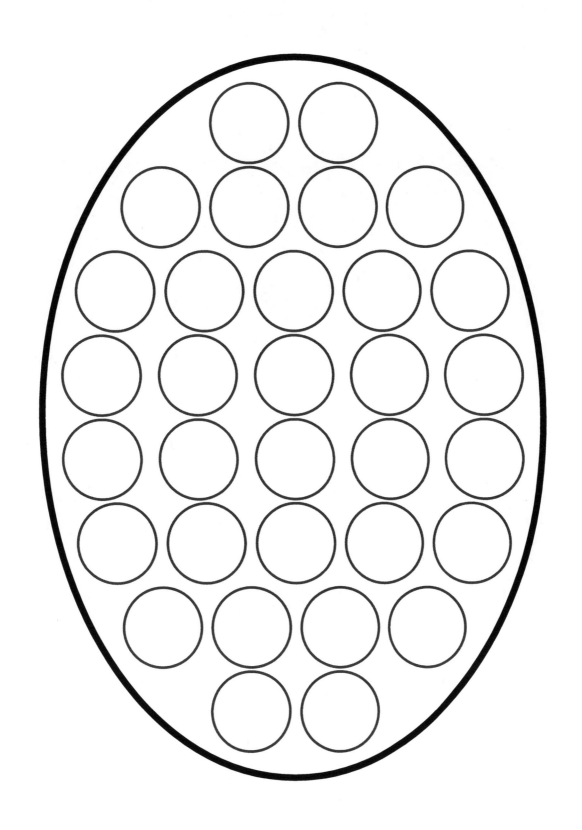

OVAL

RECTANGLE

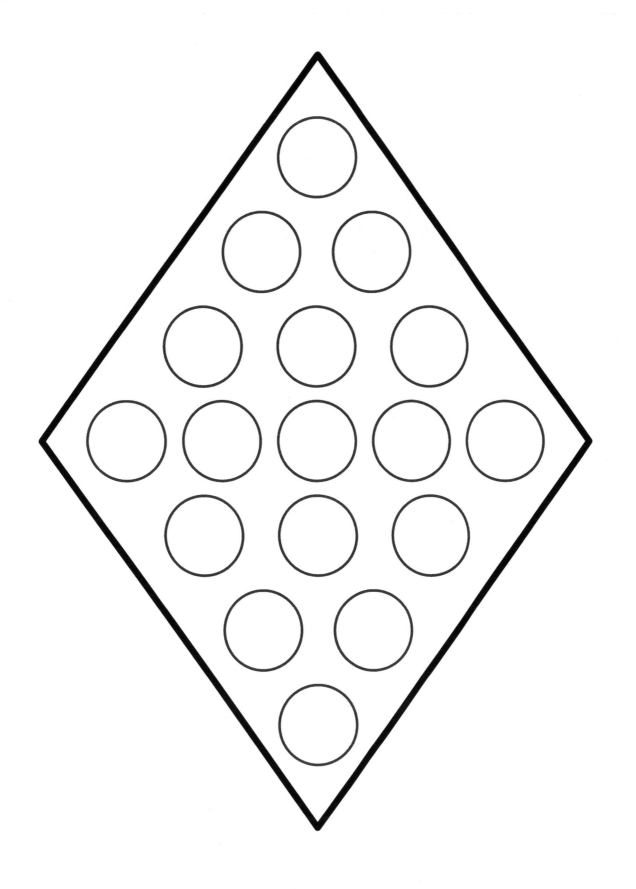

DIAMOND

HEART

STAR

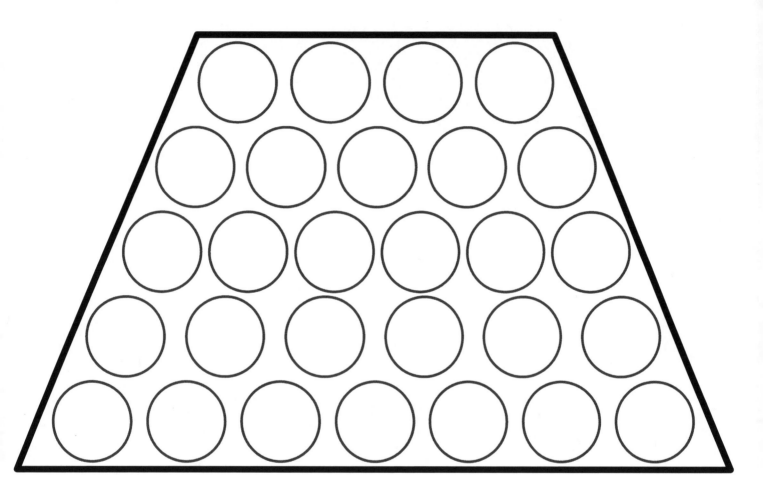

TRAPEZOID

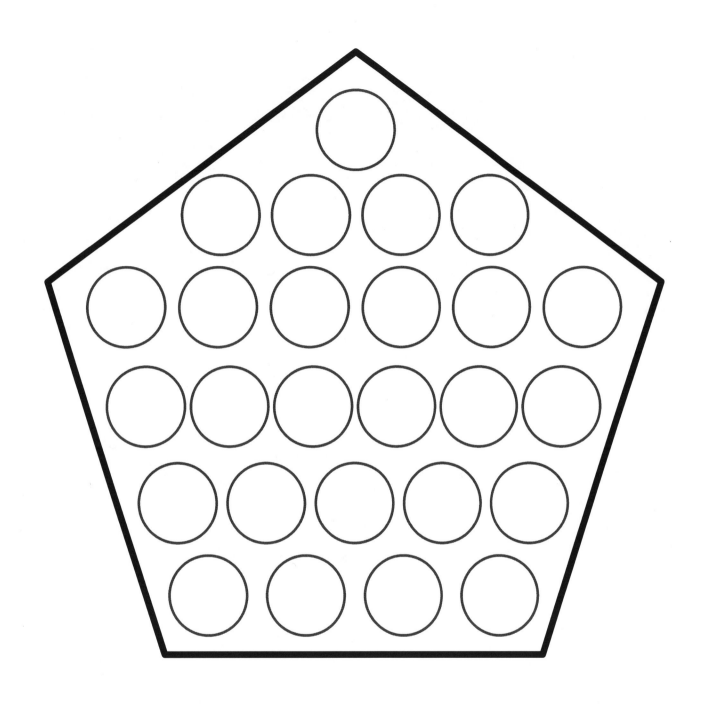

PENTAGON

DOT ONE 1

○ ○ ① ○ ○ ○ ○ ①
① ○ ○ ○ ① ○ ① ○
○ ○ ○ ① ○ ○ ○ ○
○ ① ○ ○ ① ○ ① ○
○ ○ ○ ① ○ ○ ○ ①
○ ① ○ ○ ○ ○ ① ○
○ ○ ① ○ ① ○ ○ ○
○ ○ ① ○ ○ ① ○ ①

DOT
TWO 2

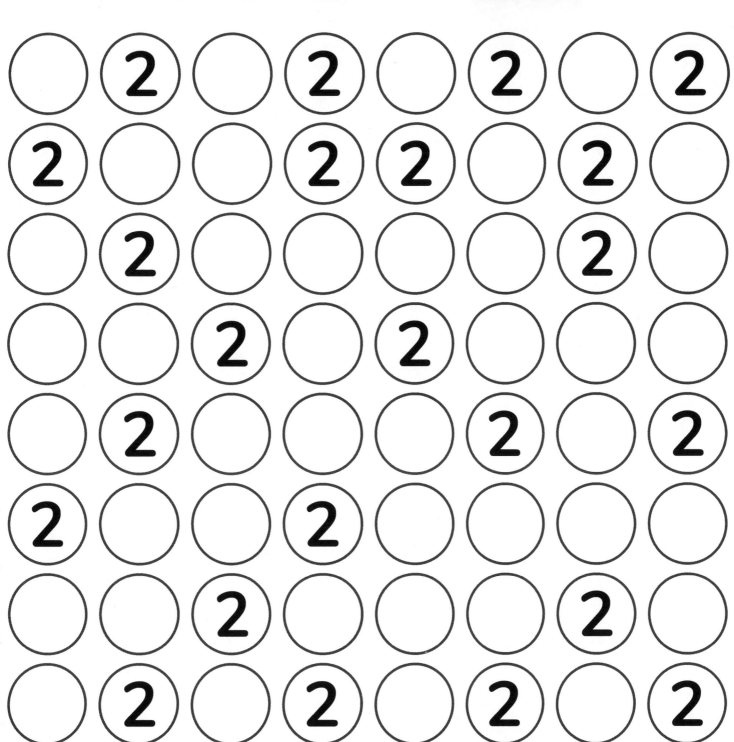

DOT
THREE 3

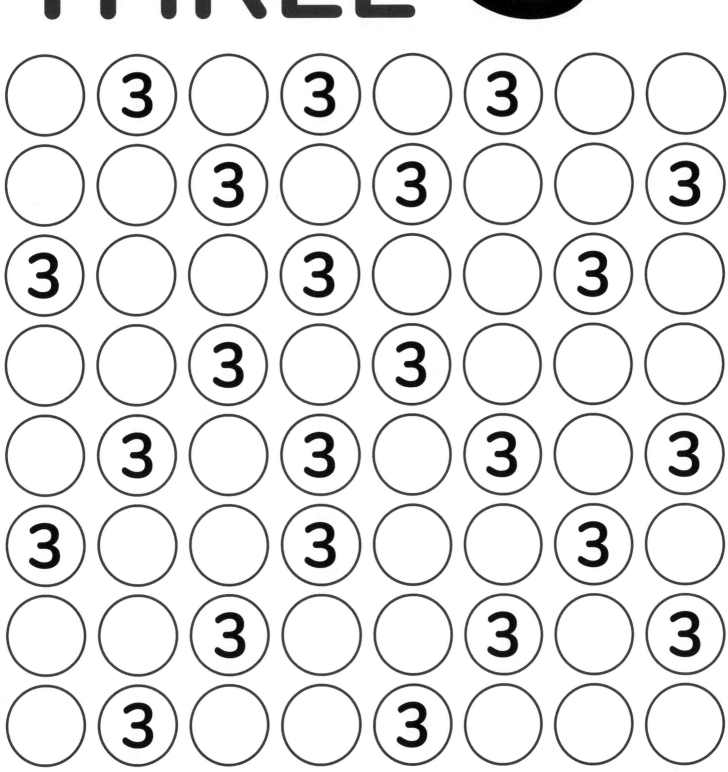

DOT
FOUR 4

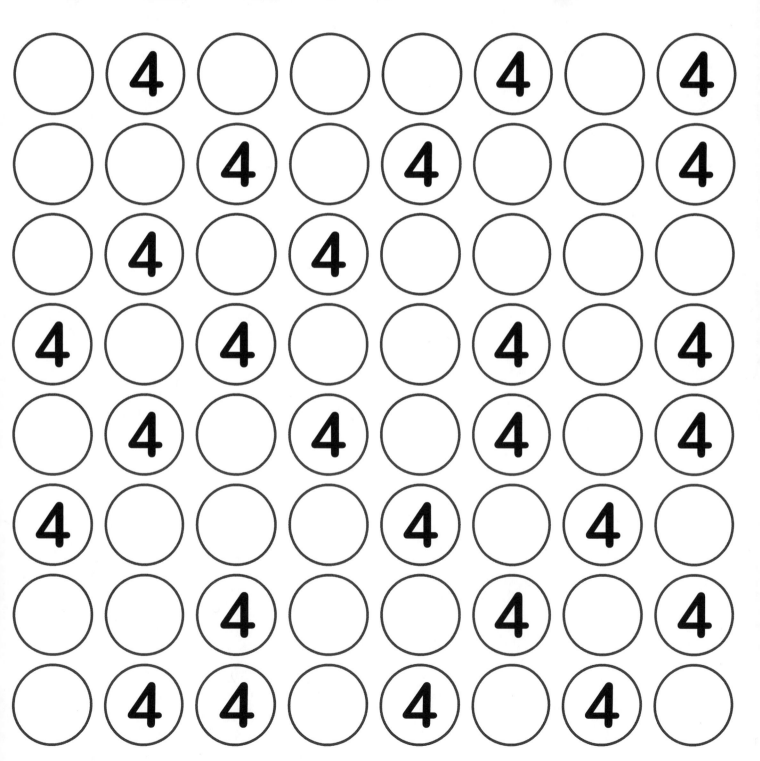

DOT
FIVE
5

5 5 5 5

5 5 5 5

5 5 5 5

5 5 5 5

5 5 5 5

5 5 5 5

5 5 5 5

5 5 5 5

DOT

SIX

6

DOT
SEVEN 7

DOT
EIGHT

8

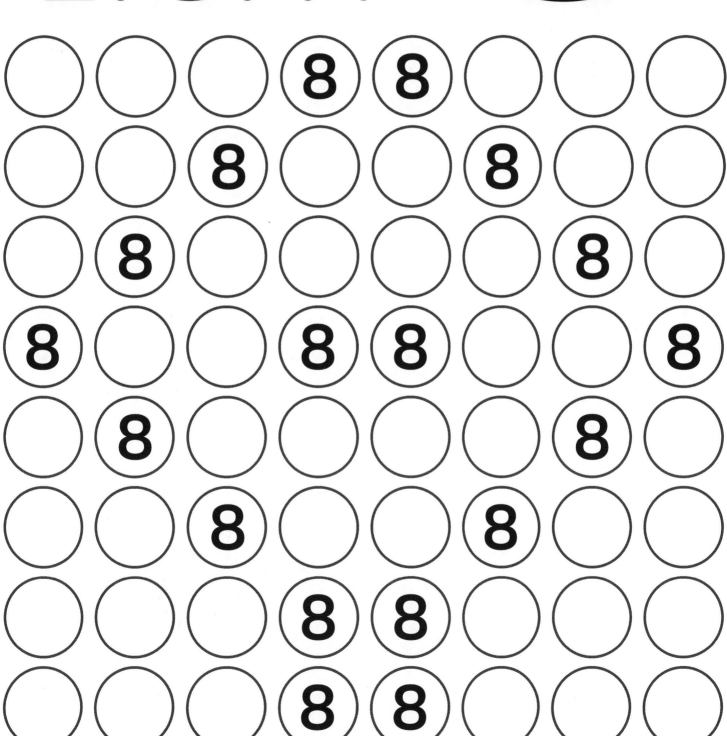

DOT
NINE 9

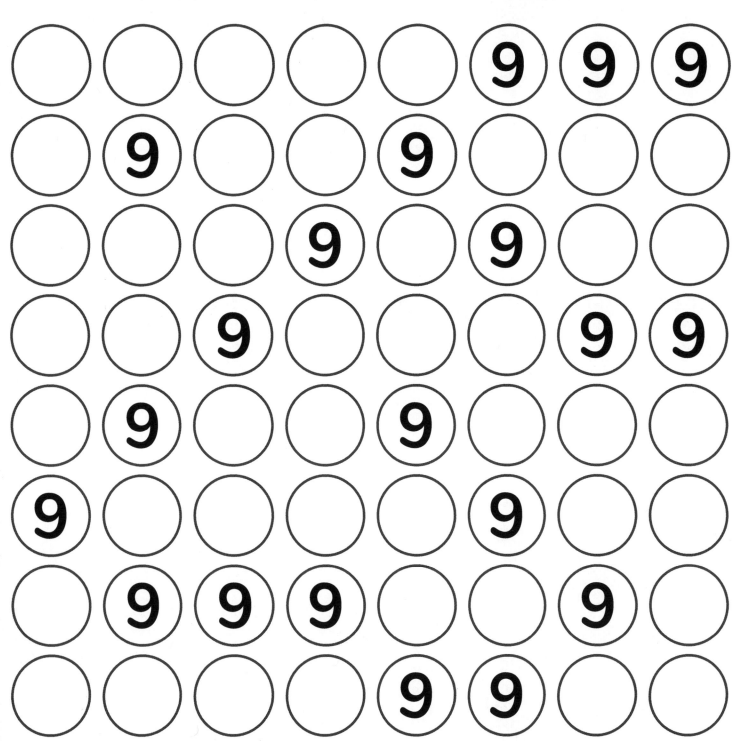

DOT

TEN 10

10　　10

10　10　10　10　10　10

10　　10　10　　10

10　　　　　　10

10　　10　10　　10

10　　　　　10

10　　10

10　10　10　10

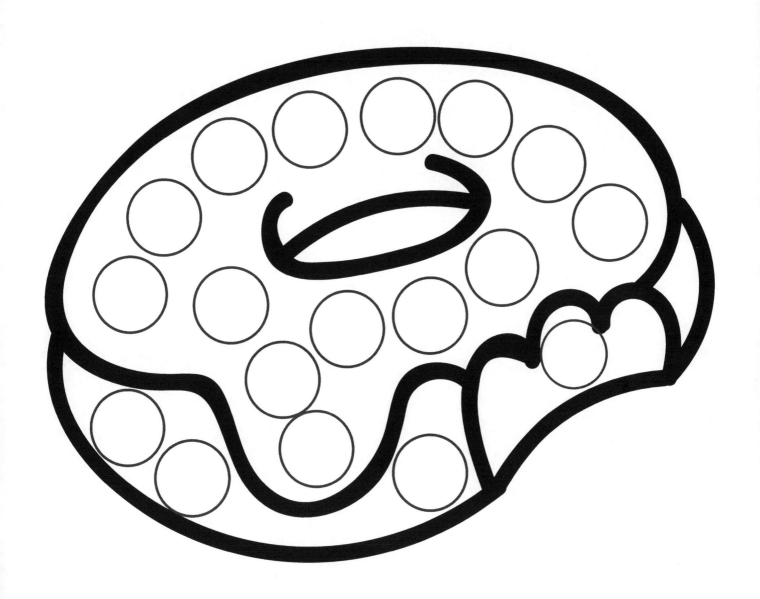

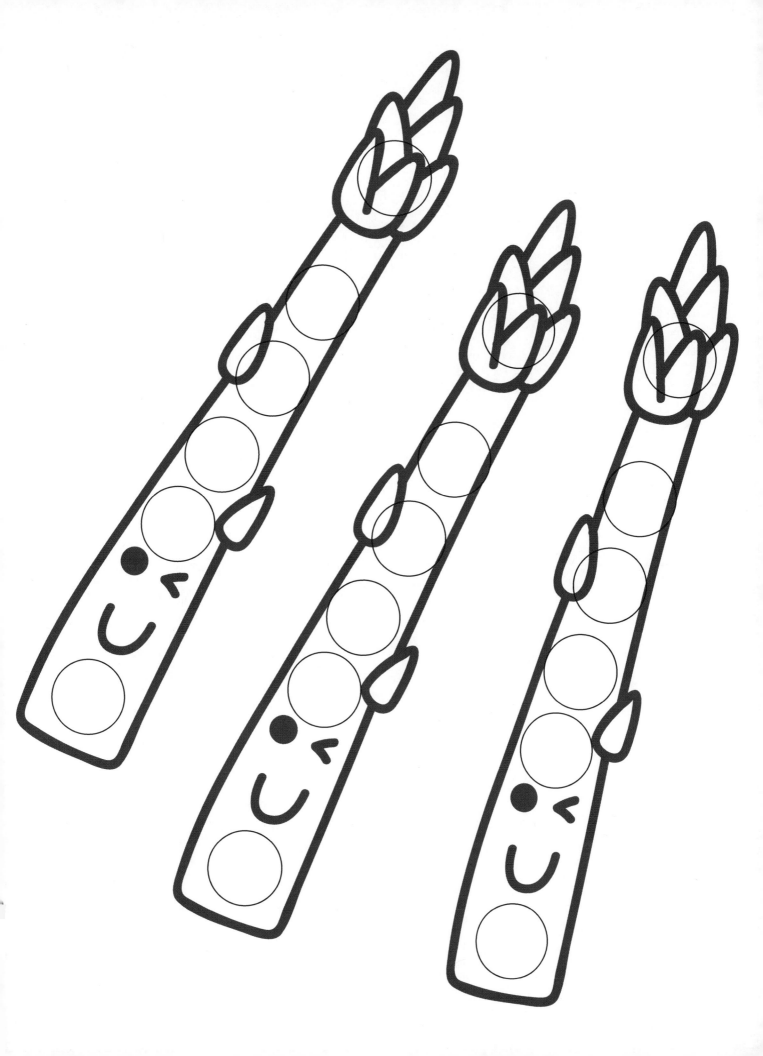

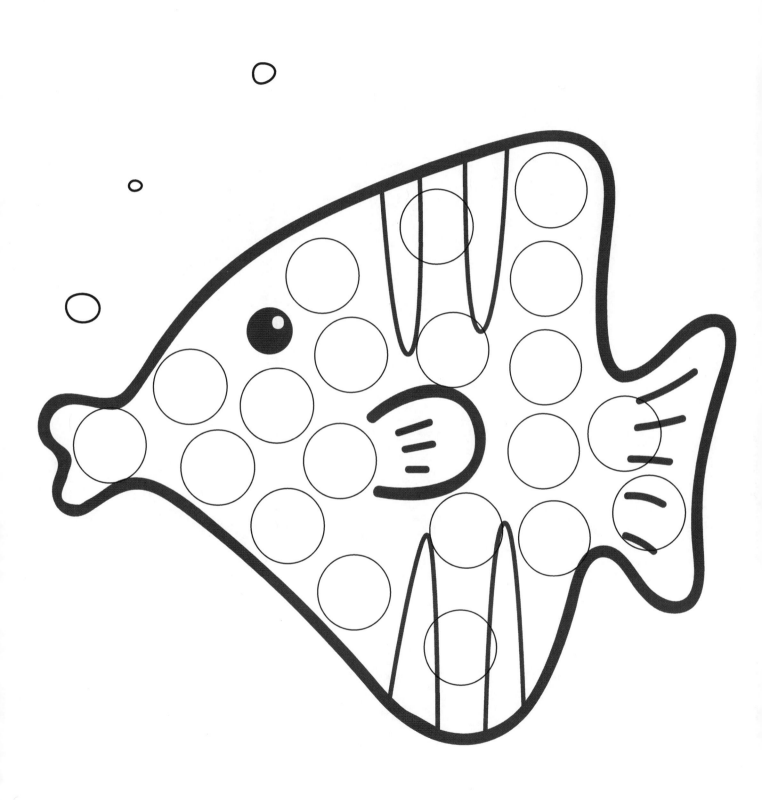

Dot Your Style

Dot Your Style

Dot Your Style

Made in the USA
Middletown, DE
07 March 2021